THE SCIENCE OF AMBITION:

Getting things done right and making a better life for yourself

By

Tara G. Pearson

TABLE OF CONTENT

CHAPTER 1:

WHAT EXACTLY IS AMBITION

Your desire to succeed is the fire that is ready to be utilized, to drive you ahead at top speed. It is the intense desire to accomplish, own, be, and have a more fulfilling life. It may take precedence over both resources and skill, making it one of the most crucial weapons for success. The concept of "success" may vary from person to person and from country to culture, but the message is always the same: setting goals and having the willpower to achieve them is crucial.

Ambitious individuals work hard and stay focused to succeed in both their personal and professional life. As they labor toward their objectives, they are inspired by an inner drive.

It is common to have periods of lower ambition in life, whether as a result of a change in employment or a change in perspective. However, going to a therapist may be a fantastic approach to understand why you're feeling less ambitious as well as work out the best strategy to enhance your ambition to get back on track if it's harming your happiness and wellness.

The Reality of Ambition:

We've all had instances when we lacked ambition. Even the world's most successful individuals sometimes experience failure and insecurity. However, even after failure, rejection, and disappointment, they finally achieve because their desire has returned. When confronted with a setback, it is simple to give up, yet having desire means getting back up when you fall.

The quality of ambition is not innate. It may be learned and developed, just like any other admirable quality. Without a doubt, one can overcome a lack of ambition. Ironically, overcoming a lack of ambition may need some ambition on your part. You are after all establishing a goal to accomplish it. Thankfully, searching for strategies to increase your ambition is a positive beginning. However, it requires perseverance and determination, and depending on what you want to do, it can take three weeks, three months, or even three years.

Being unambitious or being ambitious in ways that aren't necessarily focused on money might bring about a great deal of satisfaction (ambitious for experiences, seeing the world, developing better friendships and relationships, or having fun). But there are some intriguing traits that skilled celebrity photographers have in common, which we shall explore.

Frequently asked questions regarding ambition:

Is Losing Ambition Normal?
It is common to lose motivation for many reasons, therefore yes, this is normal. Since the COVID-19 epidemic struck in 2020, many of us have had trouble staying motivated. Many

individuals found it difficult to keep working toward their objectives in the face of persistent uncertainty about the future, or they burned out from the many demands of pandemic life.

The pursuit of something out of external drive rather than internal desire, underlying concerns, and mental health issues like depression are other variables that might lead to a loss of ambition. It might be unnerving to think that your ambition has decreased with time. Consult a mental health professional if you're worried about a continuous lack of drive or motivation; they can help you analyze your thoughts and decide what to do next.

Does Ambition Decrease with Age?

People often get less motivated as they age. When we initially enter the workforce, we can look for contentment in a certain level of financial achievement or professional accomplishment. But as we become older, we could start putting more importance on things like starting a family or other joyous events. Perhaps the definition of ambition changes as we mature and develop new ideas on pleasure and success.

CHAPTER 2:

AMBITION TYPES

1. Natural or Intrinsic Ambition

The pioneers, the risk-takers, and the people who put their necks on the line because "they have to" are innately ambitious. They could be held captive by their feelings, their morals, or their need to make a point. They want to accomplish things because it increases their feeling of self-worth, desires, and purpose.

For instance, a writer who concentrates on objectives that are important to them personally is motivated by the desire to produce the things they want to make, and their talent or motivation alone determines whether they will succeed. Goals don't depend on other people or things to define or verify their achievements.

All of these objectives center on pursuing or doing something that has personal significance for you. These objectives support the fundamental desires and needs that make up your personality. They relate to your essential beliefs, interests, and hobbies as well as to your relationships and personal development.

Your fundamental human requirements for relatedness, competence, and autonomy are met by intrinsic aims. Goals for relationships, personal development, physical health, self-acceptance, and contribution are among them.

2. Extrinsic Ambition

Extrinsically ambitious people look at what has already been accomplished and search for examples and pathways to follow so that they may achieve as well. They work inside the framework. Their success will be produced by the system.

For instance, a musician is driven by external incentives like accolades, charts, money, and the desire for fame. These aspirations fuel their job, and whether they succeed in fulfilling them will determine their level of success.

Extrinsic ambition aims to assist you in achieving an objective independent of yourself. They often center on acquiring the affirmation and acceptance of others or outside indications of one's value. They are about enhancing your public image, being wealthy, famous, or gaining control over others.

Extrinsic objectives differ from intrinsic goals in that they are entirely focused on the reward after the journey. They fixate on achieving a goal while entirely ignoring the steps used to get there.
Someone who is intrinsically driven sees things as a means to an end. The key is to arrive "there." The goal is the result, not the method.

In actuality, I believe that most of us carry a little of both, but we tend to concentrate more on one than the other.

You are pursuing extrinsic objectives, or are extrinsically ambitious if your activities are motivated by your desire to get wealthy, improve your self-image, impress others, or gain fame.

You are intrinsically driven, or more accurately, inherently ambitious, if you strive to improve yourself, learn, grow, give back to your community, or strengthen your relationships.

In general, intrinsic objectives contribute to great psychological health since they improve happiness, self-esteem, levels of happiness, and energy.

You're in danger if you just care about being wealthy, well-liked, and a "success" in society's eyes. Pursuing these extrinsic objectives might prevent you from ever experiencing true happiness and fulfillment, which makes them highly risky.

You see, pursuing these objectives distracts you from the pursuit of intrinsic goals that might benefit you. Therefore, they keep you occupied.

They continue to encourage you to chase after new, shiny things like money, automobiles, trips, recognition, and acceptance. Additionally, you could even believe that your life is improving (and in a way you are).

The issue is that this problem has no solution. There is always more material. More money can always be made. More bling may always be purchased. Always try to impress someone else. Always more, more, more... You search outside of yourself for happiness, the ultimate objective, forgetting that pleasure can only come from inside, from pursuing intrinsic and gratifying goals.

The majority of successful individuals, like Steve Jobs, Bill Gates (the Microsoft founder), Warren Buffet, Mark Cuban, Mark Twain, and others, are driven by internal motivation.

According to multi-billionaire Warren Buffett, "Making money is not our driving objective; rather, it is a by-product of that mission. Making money is usually a result of doing something you love since you're more inclined to give it all you've got.

In contrast to extrinsic objectives, intrinsic goals will result in MORE money, fame, power, validation, and approbation.

It is real. People who pursue intrinsic goals—those who simply do things for enjoyment and fulfillment—become more "extrinsically successful" than those who genuinely strive for extrinsic success.

We could find ourselves pursuing extrinsic objectives for a cause. We may resort to extrinsic objectives when our fundamental needs for autonomy, relatedness, and competence aren't being addressed.

We begin pursuing superficial ambitions as a type of defense mechanism when we feel like we can't do anything well, when we're lonely, when we don't have meaningful connections, or when we feel like we're being dominated by others around us.

Consider this. if you have all of your requirements. if you had a positive outlook on life and yourself. if you have solid connections. If you genuinely felt content and contented. if your life already consisted of nothing but great. If only everything was ideal. If you were living each day to the fullest, then...

If all of that were true, achieving success in terms of money or notoriety would not even cross one's mind. When you're already brimming over with love and happiness, why would you need anything else? That would be a ridiculous idea, isn't it?

But when our wants aren't completely satisfied, we begin seeking fulfillment from things outside of ourselves.

At that point, we begin persuading ourselves that if we could only become wealthy, well-known, or successful, we would then finally feel accepted, deserving, competent, and valued. Once we've "arrived," we'll experience a feeling of freedom, competency, and connectedness.

Newsflash: The concept of "making it" doesn't exist. There is always more money to be produced, more automobiles to be purchased, more people to impress, and more celebrities to be gained, as I previously said. It never ends, it never satisfies our fundamental wants as human beings, and it never brings us joy.

It's time to start prioritizing our requirements... It's time to begin chasing intrinsic objectives... obey your gut instinct... implement your passions... learn to like the procedure... the ability to enjoy the voyage Put all of our focus on the process and let go of the result.

CHAPTER 3: WHO OR WHAT POWERS YOUR AMBITION ?

Ambition is that flammable energy you possess that is just waiting to be used. Ambition has always served as a source of energy for me. A Ferrari of passion, desire, drive, and conviction is waiting to take off inside of me with only a little touch. The intense desire to be, have, accomplish, and experience something better in life is known as ambition. Since it triumphs over both skill and wealth, I think it is the most crucial weapon for success. No matter what is in front of them, ambition may make anybody succeed. You may achieve more in life if you have the desire and the determination, bravery, and ambition to rule the world.
Ambition is fueled by:

1. Enthusiasm / Passion
All forms of success start with desire. While ambition directs your desire in the direction of the goals you have in mind, passion comes from

the sheer pleasure of doing something. The attitude that drives us to accomplish goals is called ambition. To know what that something is, one must be passionate, which is where passion comes into play. Passion is that inner emotion and drives to bring about a certain outcome.

Since passion is an inside experience, attempting to articulate it is challenging. We strive for that goal we envision in the future and would dearly want to realize it for ourselves and for others we love.

For me, passion comes before ambition because, without passion, striving for greatness seems pointless.

When I was younger, my ambition lacked focus. I was aware that I want achievement, but I was unsure of my goals. As I grew older and began to experience life, I used self-reflection to understand myself much better and finally found a passion.

My desire was directed and channeled by this enthusiasm, allowing me to put it to good use. I managed to channel that drive and steer in the right directions rather than just being overly ambitious about everything. Your passion becomes a thing when you have ambition. It transforms your enthusiasm from something you feel in your heart into the willpower to take the necessary steps to get the outcomes you want. Your ambition will get more fervent the more passionate you are about anything. You must firmly believe that you love what you do. The impossible becomes achievable when one has a strong sense of enthusiasm and drive.

Always keep in mind that passion will help men transcend their flaws and failings.

Passion is necessary since everyday work is required to accomplish high objectives in life. Being consistent in your efforts will help. You won't be successful if you lack this constancy. For me, consistency is the key characteristic that separates successful individuals from failed ones. This holds everywhere.

Athletes who are inconsistent in their training and lack the daily drive to improve themselves will never become great champions. If a musician doesn't sing and practice every day to advance, they won't be successful.

You may conceive something so fantastic that it just could come true if you have ambition, which is your passion, drive, and love for what you do. Take Jeff Bezos for example. He had an idea for a shop where everything would be sold! And that's the birth of Amazon.

This is simply one successful entrepreneur among many others, and it serves as proof that every aspirant needs a desire to push forward. Each individual has to have a fundamental conviction that drives them on even when others don't share their outlook.

A new firm needs passion and ambition to develop and succeed, and executives should support all workers in being as ambitious as they can be. Aspiration should be utilized to stand out and emphasize one's advantages.

2. Empathy:

Giving is the key to life. Making a better "us" should be the focus of life rather than "me." Care is the cornerstone of a life well lived. You find the deeper purpose and happiness you seek via caring. What you provide to the world is what defines true success. Your ambition is sparked when you are passionate about what you are doing. You go to considerable lengths to ensure that whatever you are endorsing will have a favorable effect on other people's life. You are innately ambitious when you care about the greater picture. It will hit you personally when you witness the effect you can make and how your enthusiasm benefits others. This will only serve to feed your desire to do more and give more.

Never forget that working from your heart and changing the world is the greatest reward there is.

3. Purpose.

A clear purpose provides you the drive to make the necessary sacrifices to live the life you want.

Your compass is set by your objective. Your every thought, deed, and action is directed by it. A purpose offers you direction and enables you to manage and channel your desire in the right ways. You start to feel motivated by the dedicated, passionate, and influential person you are becoming as you start to enjoy the satisfaction of shaping and attaining your broader goal. You are unable to imagine any excuse for giving up or for failing to believe in who you are and what you stand for because of the feelings of satisfaction and excitement around your mission. Your aspirations turn your mission into a dynamic, expanding, and ongoing personal mythology.

Never lose sight of the fact that you were sent on this planet to be your best self, to fulfill your mission, and to do so bravely.

You'll have a feeling of clarity unlike any other when you properly understand your purpose because you'll be able to link the goals you have with your ultimate satisfaction. You'll experience enthusiasm, motivation, and laser-like concentration. The best gift you can give yourself is to quit fighting with the past and the future and begin living in the now.

4. Success

The desire to succeed in itself is a powerful driver of ambition. You want to succeed so that you can feel and appear successful. Rewards are crucial. This includes the benefits, advantages, and distinctions success bestows upon you. Think of your life as an obstacle course, and completing it effectively is the same as being successful. If you don't have the attitude to win from the beginning, you won't give it your all and will falter when things become challenging or complex.

The ambition required to prevail will be there when your desire for success is strong. You're willing to go to any lengths to get over your uncertainties and apparent limitations. If you're ambitious and resourceful, you'll discover alternative methods to achieve rather than giving up.

5. Fear.

The drive to commit your life to hard effort, refining your trade, sleepless nights, and sacrifice to have the life you want is sparked by a profound craving for accomplishment that is accompanied by anticipatory terror. You are driven to put in a lot of effort and perform at your best because you want to accomplish. You must want success as much as you desire air to achieve your long-term objectives. You must be prepared to overcome and endure failure-related worries. Your ability to achieve will only be as strong as the daily adjustments you are willing to make in your life.

There are no shortcuts, and your determination alone will enable you to overcome your worries and pursue your goals. Put everything on the line and never let an idea pass you by. You must make the most of these opportunities to ensure that your time is spent moving you ever-closer to your ambition.

You must walk through fear, not around it, to overcome it.

6. Retaliation

Human nature makes others want you to fail. People will happily gloat about your failure rather than your success. It's an unavoidable reality. There are two methods to reply to those who are trying to tear you down by criticizing you: One is to withdraw and worry that you could fail; the other is to seize your desire and make sure you achieve despite the doubters. Your success and pleasure are the best presents you can offer to others who are unsure, critical, jealous, and negative. Use their criticism to motivate you and keep you focused on your goals.

The finest retaliation is an enormous success.

Short-term victories help you to realize that achievement is the greatest kind of retaliation and to justify your existence. Just show the doubters they are incorrect rather than engaging in verbal sparring.

Never accept average in this life. Being elite By associating yourself with your goal, you agreed to experience both highs and lows. Your personal growth, lessons, joy, and spectacular success are all contained within the journey. You'll learn through your ambition that your hardships, grit, and conflicts are gifts. The secret to ultimate success in life is found on the inside, not on the outside. It originates from your feeling of self-worth, which you can never acquire from anybody else. To continue developing and pushing yourself, to achieve more and offer more than is convenient or even considered feasible, you must leverage what motivates your desire. The individual who values life, improves the lives of others, is appreciative, and is motivated to make a difference is the richest person on earth.

I've grown to feel that ambition is the most essential and holy aspect of who we are. To accept our own calling as our souls have called us is to feel ambition and act on it. To not pursue that goal would be to reject who we are and the reason we are here.

CHAPTER 4: QUALITIES OF VERY AMBITIOUS INDIVIDUALS

We all want to succeed and struggle to do so. However, if success was effortless, we would all be achieving the same levels of success. Success is elusive, which is what makes pursuing it so remarkable. Success has ultimately shown to be a privilege enjoyed by a small number of individuals. Those are the folks that went above and above in their life to achieve where they are now. They didn't achieve success because they were fortunate or because it was given to them. They have the unadulterated desire required to attain the accomplishments they have.

1. Ability to make a sacrifice

You won't attain the degree of achievement you want without putting in a lot of effort and being ready to grind it out. Your input will equal your result, therefore you must adhere to the fundamental principles of success. You must give up a lot of the things that are a part of a typical existence if you want to live an unusual and amazing one.

Be prepared to execute oneself with all of your heart and soul, without hoping for good fortune. Never anticipate fortuitous breaks; instead, work for them. You can't rely on chance. Without sacrifice, there can be no advancement or success, and a man's success in the world will depend on how much he is willing to give up. Embrace your interests to the point that your toil doesn't feel like toil. Eat, sleep, and drink them. Be the best version of yourself. Nothing can stop you when your attention is concentrated.

You can never reach your ultimate degree of achievement if you are not prepared to give up your ego, conveniences, or security. Your amount of achievement is closely correlated with the level of sacrifice you make. You must devote a tremendous amount of time to reading, studying, and experimentation if you want to create an empire. If you binge-watch Netflix and frequently oversleep, you can't accomplish that.

You must put in a ton of sweat, effort, and time working out if you want to have a rock-hard, toned figure. If you continue to eat an unhealthy, poisonous diet of alluring junk food, you cannot do it.

Sacrifice is difficult. Nobody promised it would be simple. However, every great success comes with a great price.

2. Inquisitiveness and a desire to learn.

Most people are obstinate with the opinion that they are fully informed. You are prevented from realizing your full potential by this narrow focus. Learn something new every day and explore new things to be radically successful. Be curious about problems, not defeated by them. Ask questions to get new information. Read, go to seminars and hire a business coach. Curiosity is critical to your success because it's the strong desire to learn without constraint, it signals a hungry mind. If you're inquisitive, you're open to new experiences. It is the impetus behind discoveries across many disciplines, not just science and technology.

Every excellent thing begins with excitement or a desire to accomplish it. The same is true with success tales. The road to success becomes more obvious the more you push yourself to be educated and willing to learn.

According to research, curiosity not only aids in professional success but also enhances memory and learning.
Undoubtedly, you cannot expect yourself to be naturally motivated to learn new things or to achieve if you do not have a real desire or curiosity to study. Your success begins with a desire to learn new things. Remember that new scientific discoveries that have enhanced our everyday lives are the result of scientists' natural curiosity and desire to learn more.

Success is built upon knowledge. You must always be hungry for new knowledge, education, and learning if you want to achieve. Your job becomes easier the more you know. Transform all of your newly acquired information into expertise and put it to use. You may fully benefit from what you have learned in this manner.

3. Creation of trusting friendships.
Your social circle is a direct reflection of your financial standing. To succeed, you don't have to be loud, haughty, or attention-seeking. The elite who are successful prefer to work quietly and let their achievements speak for themselves. You must always network with people in a mature, intelligent, and classy manner. Exchange facts, discuss concepts and happenings, and always address individuals by their first names.

Make use of proximity by forming connections with groups of prosperous individuals.
Create a contact list of individuals who will return your calls and appreciate your relationship, ideas, and hobbies. In today's world, it all comes down to who you know and how you can support one another in achieving your goals.

Expose yourself to successful individuals if you want to succeed. Take advice from their experiences and emulate their behavior. The nice byproduct of imitating success is that it replicates your life.

Developing solid connections opens doors to new possibilities, enhances our creative intelligence, and promotes progress.

4. Enthusiastic about personal development.

Ambitious people are never satisfied with their life circumstances. They are eager to explore the possibilities for their future. You have to adopt this personality type. Be constantly looking for ways to examine and improve all aspects of your life, including your intellect, heart, health, and time management. Work tirelessly to develop your personality, managerial abilities, and every other aspect of your life. You must work to correct any shortcomings in yourself that you cannot accept.

Personal development is a component of personal growth. That entails investing in oneself so that they can successfully manage themselves, no matter what obstacles life throws at them.

Tips for self-growth: Read new books, learn a new hobby, Overcome your fear, Level up your skill, Wake up early, Have a weekly exercise routine, Get out of your comfort zone, Compete with yourself, Set goals, Acknowledge your flaws, Get into the action, Learn from people that inspire you, Quit bad habits and embrace good ones, Get a mentor, Learn to deal with difficult people, Meditate, Learn chess game, Take a break, Let go of the past.

5. Creativity or Originality.

"Those who rush with the throng frequently get lost in it," is a wise proverb. Ambitious people do not follow the herd. Be fervent in your desire to challenge the existing quo. Examine unconventional ideas and thinking. Take a chance and expect rejection. Success often results from deviating from the usual. Repeating what has previously been done won't ever lead to something worthwhile.

The inventive brains of the ambitious never end. Always ask the question, "Why not?" Being creative allows you to identify opportunities when others perceive a dead end. You suddenly wake up in the middle of the night to write down an idea you had because you want to examine and develop it the following day. A creative mind like this has the power to alter the course of history.

Humans are naturally creative, but as they become older, they are educated to be uncreative. When you're young, you're encouraged to "reach for the skies" and attend art lessons, but as you grow older, you're advised to get real, follow the straight and narrow road, and pay your taxes.

6. Independent and trustworthy.

There is no space for making excuses or attempting to place the blame or responsibility for your difficulties on others when you are driven by desire. If you are having trouble, remember that you are the factor that unites all of your experiences and humble yourself. You are where all change starts and ends.

Use your desire to accept full responsibility for your present situation if you want to succeed in the way you see yourself succeeding. Be innovative and problem-focused. Change your behavior and rely primarily on yourself to complete tasks. Avoid becoming or becoming trapped. Make choices, then proceed. To succeed, you must accept full responsibility for your actions. Always take the effort to check if you are moving on the path you believe you are meant to travel.

7. Keep Perspective:

Notwithstanding the number of the pressure or chaos you face every day, control your ambition and maintain balance. Learn to breathe easily and relax. You can breathe easier when you can maintain perspective. To concentrate on solutions rather than problems, slow down. This enables you to make wise selections and the appropriate inquiries even in difficult situations. Things start to go south when you let your emotions control you. The obstacles of life and business are like an obstacle course. You need to be a competent problem solver and not focus on just one specific obstacle if you want to be successful. Your aspiration necessitates continuous movement.

8. The time is "Now".

The only moment you have that you are directly in control of is "now." Give your desire to the task at hand. Spend no time dwelling on what has already been accomplished. Make the most of every second of this present moment to achieve your potential and succeed. To prevent making the same errors again, you must decide to draw lessons from the past and apply those lessons to the present. What you are doing right now will determine your future.

9. React quickly.

What you desire is constantly within reach thanks to technological advancements. Be the first and fastest to seize any chance that comes your way. Take hold of each one of them. Avoid letting things drag on or taking too long to react to changes that may present themselves. You don't want your rivals to seize an opportunity from you as a result of your tardy answer. Time is of the essence, therefore take advantage of your desire to elicit quick reactions.

10. Never give up.

I like challenges. When times are tough at work, persevere. When a task becomes too difficult, the afraid give up, while the ambitious use the difficulty as a chance to expand their knowledge, abilities, and perspectives. You must realize that if success were simple, everyone would experience it without any effort. To overcome your present difficulty, you must be prepared to give up any out-of-date views you may have. Make it your mission to win every time.

The majority of those who have achieved success in our world began from the bottom and rose to the top because of their intense desire. It's only when you're at the right place at the right moment that luck enters the picture, but it's up to you to reach where you're going. Being successful is all about how much you want something and are prepared to work for it; it's about your drive to get it.

CHATER 5: TIPS FOR IGNITING YOUR AMBITION

When paired with a strong sense of resolve, this kind of motivation enables you to do everything you set your mind to and to succeed in every endeavor. Of course, every quality that seems to be favorable in general has drawbacks. While ambition helps us stay motivated, focused, and engaged with our goals, objectives, and aspirations, it may also lead to self-involvement and avarice if it becomes excessive.

Finding the correct balance is crucial if we want our desire to drive us passionately toward our objectives. If you are having trouble being ambitious, hang in there. We've all experienced times when we lacked drive and ambition, but developing drive and ambition is a process that can be learned. All it takes is commitment, concentration, perseverance, and hard work.

Tips for igniting your desire and moving on to achievement:

- ## Set objectives

Setting goals for yourself is one of the most crucial things you can do since without them, you won't know whether or not you've accomplished something you can be proud of. Set a challenging objective for yourself and provide some interim benchmarks. Be specific about your goals, including the timeframe for achieving them. Remember to picture your objectives as well. When you imagine something and put it in your head, you'll be surprised at how much you can do.

Don't simply sit back and be lazy if you're having trouble with your motivation and desire right now; push yourself instead. There are several ways to challenge yourself, like starting your podcast, writing your book, setting a new objective for your spiritual or physical health, or posting material on tik-tok.

There is never a better moment to push yourself than right now since it is preferable to binge-watching mindless television or berating Covid-19.

- **Don't be afraid to take chances.**
You must take risks and feel at ease with them if you want to feed your desire. Yes, there may be instances when you need to take a risk or stake everything on a single choice. But more often than not, you'll come to know that your worst fear won't come true. You must allow yourself the opportunity to try new things and consider a wide range of possibilities if you want to become more ambitious. The next big chance might be just around the corner from you. You just need to try. You must learn to withstand fear and anxiety if you want to achieve more, so be prepared to face them.

The adage "the greatest risk generates the greatest profit" is true for a reason. It's because every innovative concept carries some level of danger. Along your path through life, you'll encounter challenging choices. Be willing to take risks as a result.

• Get Rid of the Negative

The adversary is negativity, plain and simple. Negativity holds us back and obscures the opportunities that lie ahead, whether it originates from the outside or the inside. Reaching your objectives seems like you've placed a large, ominous cloud over it. Remove negativity, don't criticize yourself, don't compare yourself to others, and keep your attention on yourself. Work on improving yourself and your objectives; be committed to your goals, and keep the big picture in mind. No one else is your primary rival; it is you. Focus on the good and strive to be better today than you were yesterday.

• Spend money on yourself

The most significant and valuable investment you can make in your life is in yourself, therefore put money into yourself and believe in your value. Also bear in mind that investing in yourself requires more than just financial resources. It involves setting aside time for yourself, engaging in regular exercise, getting eight hours of sleep each night, eating a wholesome, well-balanced diet, learning something new, developing the right relationships, and nourishing your mind with motivating, energizing, and empowering books, podcasts, and movies. Put yourself first, and others will see you as such.

- **Wait no more**

You will never achieve anything if you keep waiting for the ideal situation—the ideal people, the ideal resources, the ideal time. You will never see tomorrow if you keep claiming it will. When you aren't working for greatness, you can't expect it. Being ambitious entails pushing oneself ahead, fighting for what you desire, and refusing to accept defeat. Instead of waiting for anything to happen, live your life. Get involved in the game and make things happen.

- **Be fervent.**

Any accomplishment begins with passion because it stems from a love and enthusiasm for what you are doing. On the other side, ambition propels your desire toward the goal you want to achieve. To achieve your goals, you need ambition, which turns your enthusiasm from thinking to acting. Your ambition will be more intense the more passionate you are about anything. The impossible will become achievable if you are passionate about what you do and back it up with desire.

- **Care**

Existence is not about "me," but rather about improving "us," and happy, contented life is founded on compassion. Your life will have more significance if you care, and what you offer to the world will define your ultimate success. When you care sincerely, your ambition is fueled and ignited by that energy. When you care, you are inherently more ambitious because you see the potential for good change.

- **Run Your Imagination Through It**

The power of imagination is wonderful. It is a great tool for combating pessimism and for getting away from the daily grind. Remember that when you meet a difficulty, your level of ambition decreases since ambition is a condition of being. Your imagination will be your biggest ally at this point. Encourage oneself by imagining solutions to the issues and brighter days ahead. Recognize the influence of the mind on the matter, and utilize your imagination to further your goals.

It's crucial to think creatively if you want to reach significant life objectives. Use creative solutions to tackle challenging issues. Design workable solutions using your imagination.

While it's understandable to have a clear vision for your life, keep in mind that uncertainty is a normal aspect of life. Living in denial entails allowing your expectations to be inflexible. Navigate your way around the uncertainty rather than battling it. To promote stability in your life, use creativity.

- ## **Concentrate on Acquiring Knowledge**

You have two choices for every chance. Either education or financial gain are options. But bear in mind that when you pursue profit, you could succeed or you might fail. However, you will consistently be motivated and ambitious if you seek information, learn from your experiences, experiment, explore, and develop. It maintains your attention and makes the trip worthwhile. Therefore, if you want to be ambitious, concentrate on learning from your experiences rather than making money from them, and you will improve every aspect of your life. Concentrate on developing yourself and obtaining experience. Even if you don't ask for it, praise always comes your way when you perform your work effectively.

- ## **Remain Dedicated**

Staying committed entails being ready to carry out necessary tasks even when you don't feel like it. It's the determination to never give up on a worthwhile endeavor. Yes, dedication might be difficult under difficult situations, but it is necessary to support your desire. Be prepared to give up momentary pleasures to attain your goals. Establish a rigid timetable for yourself to keep you accountable. This will encourage you to be ambitious and driven as you go on.

In reality, there are no such things as overnight successes. Even then, it's simple to arrive and simple to depart. Construct a lifetime journey in your thoughts from the minute you decide to pursue a desire. Nothing good ever occurs in a split second.

If you feed your ambition, there are no boundaries for you. You may do more in life and bring about the good changes you want by setting objectives, making an action plan, and remaining committed. Fear won't stop you from doing these things. Sure, there may be days when you want to give up, but if you keep going, your ambitious dreams will come to fruition.

CHAPTER 6 : HOW TO DEAL WITH A LACK OF AMBITION

There are several actions you may do to increase your ambition or instill ambition where none previously existed if you feel like "I'm losing my ambition." You may carry out these actions yourself or with your mental health provider's assistance.

1. Look for a mentor.

Finding a role model whose success closely resembles what you aspire to accomplish will help you find the motivation to continue pursuing your objectives. It can be a coworker or a different individual that you admire.

Numerous studies demonstrate the beneficial effects that mentoring relationships have on both the mentor and the mentee. Success depends on having someone you can share your expertise with or who can help you along your route since they've probably previously traveled it. Whatever your objectives may be, mentoring seems to make a difference.

Having a mentor to look up to and seek advice from can be tremendously inspiring, regardless of where your ambitions take you. Regardless of your definition of success, mentoring connections are a crucial component.

2. Set Your Goals.

Create a visual depiction of your objectives, whether it be on a whiteboard, index cards, or Pinterest board, so you can understand precisely what it is you are aiming for. A strong sense of your destination might help you stay motivated.

3. Be Active, Keep moving.

Being physically and mentally fitter via exercise might help you remain focused while you work harder to achieve your objectives. Find a hobby you like, and stay with it.

The link between physical exercise and laziness may not come as a surprise to you. In other words, you become less lazy in other areas of your life as you become more physically active. You start to strive for success in your career, in your social circles of friends or family, and your leisure activities.

The majority of successful individuals engage in daily exercise or physical activity. There are several advantages to physical activity. These benefits consist of the following:

- Development of the mind
- Feeling good about accomplishing objectives
- Improved planning and time management abilities
- Heightened competition (with yourself, not others)

In addition to these advantages, exercising and being active can improve your appearance. Despite our reluctance to acknowledge it, our appearance does have an impact on both our personal and professional achievement, therefore achieving our fitness objectives may increase our chances of success.

Your confidence and chance of success may both rise as a result of improving your appearance and self-esteem.

4. Increase Support.

You are unlikely to pursue your goals if all you see around you are people who are not doing so. Look for friends who are pursuing similar objectives.

A powerful way to ensure that you continue to be ambitious is to surround yourself with other ambitious people.

Being around successful and ambitious people will probably make you more successful and ambitious because, as you've probably heard, you tend to become like the five people you spend the most time with. You're less likely to maintain your ambition if you associate with people who lack it.

5. Develop Yourself and Your Self-Belief

Tests of your personality and aptitude may reveal a lot about you, including your goals, desires, and weaknesses. When you're experiencing low motivation, knowing yourself well can enable you to rekindle the urge to continue ahead.

You must become more self-aware and aware of your interests if you want to be an ambitious person. Use aptitude tests and conversations with people who are familiar with you to identify your inherent talents.

You'll discover what things you're already driven to accomplish when you give yourself time to figure out what makes you tick. These internal motivations may be used to help you stay motivated.
You may want to consider becoming a lawyer if you are enthusiastic about assisting others in obtaining justice. You may spend some time defending them. You may start a foundation for abandoned children if you are enthusiastic about doing so. Spend some time getting to know them and taking care of them.

You may overcome your lack of ambition by setting each of these objectives.
You are capable of overcoming challenges! Your life may be altered. Believe that you are larger than your circumstances, even if they have given you a difficult time.

6. Stop talking to yourself negatively.

Although negative self-talk may appear like you are just being truthful with yourself, its only purpose is to undermine you. Use precise, objective language while talking to yourself about yourself rather than being critical. You may substitute "You're no good at anything!" with something like "You struggled at work today, and that's alright." Tomorrow, you'll try once again.

7. Manage Your Envy.

Allow jealousy to motivate you rather than letting it trap you. If you want to travel on your own to the recent vacation your buddy had, start saving. Sit down and figure out what you need to do to acquire your own dream house if you're envious of your sibling's ability to buy one.

8. Make a list of things to do.

Writing down everything you need to get done the next day or the following week will help you clear your thoughts and give you a feeling of success each time you complete a job.

When making your to-do list, you should be mindful to maintain a positive outlook. If not, you run the danger of succumbing to the "it's too hard" trap. This trap is simple to fall into since it stems from concentrating on how far you still have to go rather than how far you've already gone. Lists of things to do may reveal both, which isn't necessarily a good thing.

You may want to hold off on making a to-do list until you've discovered something that will inspire you to maintain your goals high. To know where to start and prevent feeling overwhelmed by the list, you may wish to ask your mentor or support group for assistance while creating the list in the first place.

9. Develop Your Skills.

Everyone is skilled at something. Even if your skills don't appear very amazing at first ("Who cares if I can juggle?"), they probably include some little amount of enjoyment or use.

10. Find a Need

If you're having trouble staying motivated, consider how you might make your community better.

What need do you see for those youngsters in your community, if we stick with the abandoned children scenario from earlier? Your county doesn't have a shelter, right? Are there a lot of abandoned kids around that would benefit from shelters to live in? If you can identify a need, you may make little objectives to gradually meet it, which will keep you motivated.

11. Self-assess your priorities and create your meaning.

Determine what success means to you before you can pursue it honestly and successfully. Some individuals base their definition of success on how much money they earn, while others base it on how much time they can spend with their loved ones or engaging in their interests.

Goals and needs might vary throughout time. Maybe you value your relationship more than the profession you've always wanted. On the other hand, maybe having the family you want is less vital than landing that ideal career. Allow yourself the flexibility to alter your plans as you go. Rigidity is one of the most powerful incentive killers.

12. Consider Your Successes.

When you feel like you've lost all inspiration, keep memories of past victories close at hand. You may get out of a slump and continue working toward your objectives by thinking back on your accomplishments.

You're also more likely to understand how you accomplished your victories when you reflect on them. We often create patterns of failure or paint ourselves in a negative light when we reflect on our failures. Your capacity to discover ambition and eventually achieve your objectives depends much on how you see yourself.

13. Seek Someone to Look Up To.

Find someone whose accomplishments you can admire from afar, as opposed to a mentor who is actively engaged in your life. This might be someone with a similar background—for example, someone who overcame poverty—or someone who matches your aspirations, like someone who has achieved success in their profession in academics. On social media, even a stranger that you like might have a beneficial impact on you.

14. Dream on! and put "Abundance Mindset" into practice.

Imagine the ultimate version of your life after achieving your objectives. Even while you shouldn't live in your imagination, sometimes reveling in the anticipated results of your labors may be beneficial and inspiring. Imagine all the opportunities that might arise if you, for example, had more money, more enjoyable hobbies, or any other objective you choose to pursue.

Develop an abundant attitude by practicing it. Attempt to treat a failed relationship as a single unsuccessful relationship. Consider a setback at work for what it is—a setback. A mentality of abundance holds that there is always more to be obtained and room for progress.

15. Use your interests.

Where ambition may let you down, passion will enable you to persevere. Although passion and ambition are essentially different, both are necessary if you want to thrive in life. Because passion is about overcoming obstacles and persevering against all circumstances, it has a positive meaning. Without passion, ambition is nearly guaranteed to not exist.

Discover your passions and consider how you may use them to further your objectives. You may combine your love for painting with your desire for a teaching profession by pursuing a degree in art education. If you like cooking a lot and want to work in corporate law, you may utilize cooking as a way to unwind and relax when your burden becomes too much.

16. Look for Inspiration

You won't always feel motivated; sometimes you have to go get it. When you don't feel like getting out of bed, treat yourself by going to your preferred coffee shop. Consider all the stress-free time you'll have after the paper is completed if you decide you don't want to finish the paper for your class.

People may also choose to see motivational talks or videos at the same time to get the inspiration they need to finish a task. The appropriate approach and attitude might also be used to encourage oneself. Reading might also aid in obtaining sufficient motivation.

17. Get outside of your comfort zone.

Although they may seem comfortable, comfort zones may sometimes prevent development. Instead of staying in your comfort zone, encourage yourself to take on novel tasks and experiment with novel concepts, like learning a new language. Even failing is not the worst thing you can do.

It's not a good idea to go too far from your comfort zone either. We are more likely to give up before reaching our objectives if we significantly go outside of our comfort zone. Additionally, we are less inclined to connect with others around us. We must attain what psychologists refer to as optimum anxiety if we are to get the most value for our money.

You'll be able to work as productively as possible if you can put yourself in a state of optimum anxiety, which is when you're just a little bit outside of your comfort zone but not too far. Additionally, you'll discover that in the future it will be a lot easier for you to go outside of your comfort zone. It's easy to discover new interests and goals since creativity thrives in ideal anxiety levels.

18. Be willing to learn and respect the learning process.

Success is a journey, not an endpoint. Try to take pleasure in the process as it unfolds since there will always be another challenge and another hill. Many of us adopt the mentality that we need to move quickly and get to our destination, and as a result, we lose out on all of the opportunities to learn along the way.

After receiving your certificate or degree, learning is something you never stop doing. Spend some time each day studying something new, and look for chances to get hands-on experience with anything that even vaguely interests you. While having breakfast, read the newspaper, listen to a podcast, or just ask a friend or colleague to share some fresh information with you.

19. Never be afraid to take a single step.

Failure anxiety may paralyze you. Your thoughts may get consumed with it, and you may begin to doubt your ability to succeed. It could make you lose confidence in yourself. Your ability to achieve your goals will be hindered by all the things that a fear of failure is capable of. It could stifle your drive and lead to a circumstance where you end yourself back where you began.

Accept failure rather than dread it. Recognize that little setbacks are inevitable and that they may teach you valuable lessons as you go toward your objectives. Failure is OK as long as you maintain your attention on the positive and learn how to correct errors in the future.

To achieve your objectives, put one foot in front of the other. It is not always necessary to take a significant move, like relocating across the nation. It may just be looking into how much that relocation will cost. The task includes planning, so keep that in mind.

20. Seek Assistance.

Ask for assistance if it becomes too much, you're overworked, or there are too many demands on your time. Bring in a reliable friend, member of your family, or a colleague to help lighten your burden. Working in a team is not a sin.

21. Do your research.

It might be risky to pursue your aspirations blindly. You put yourself in danger if you go across the nation to pursue acting only to discover that you would need to work three jobs (jobs you do not have) to finance a single studio apartment. Instead, decide what measures you need to take to reach your objectives and give yourself enough time to do so.

Without research, you'll probably keep failing, and it may be the end of your desire. A crucial component of maintaining ambition is learning the measures to take to reach where you need to go, learning about the greatest locations in the world to succeed, and studying others who have achieved comparable success.

22. Daily Work on Yourself.

You'll stumble. You'll give up. But continue to improve yourself! Make sure you're cultivating traits and behaviors that you like and can be proud of even at a senior age because you're the one who will be with you every step of the way. A strong incentive is seeing yourself develop into the person you've always wanted to be.

CHAPTER 7:

OVERCOMING AMBITION'S BURDEN

There always appears to be a new book you need to read, whether it's to learn how to invest, develop your leadership abilities, or improve your emotional intelligence. Every time you get into social media, it feels like there is a lot more work to be done, whether it be finding out what kind of diet is best for your body or including exercise in your daily routine. Every time you talk to someone who has experienced success, they will tell you that there is still work to be done. Find a mentor, update your LinkedIn profile, work on your CV, build contacts with potential business partners and industry leaders, or develop your company concept.

You still need to sustain your love connections, friendships, and family ties despite all said above.

They want to do everything immediately appears to be overpowering.

Even if you have a never-ending list of things to accomplish, there always appears to be a nagging sense hanging over your head that you can't shake and that fuels your desire to achieve. You have restlessness in your daily life because you believe there is more out there but are unsure how to get there.

How to deal with success's weight;

1. Control your aspirations

Young professionals often make the mistake of letting their ambition consume them to the point that it leaves them powerless. There is a fierce desire to excel and succeed, so strong that dread begins to paralyze them. Eventually, instead of pursuing your goals actively, you come to a stop.

The first step to overcoming the excitement and dread is realizing that you own and control your goal. It gives you a sense of control and enables you to control your fear.

You must be cool-headed, in control, and able to think clearly to be productive and forward-thinking. This is accomplished by parking without "feeling hurried" and letting the procedure unfold naturally.

2. Do not belittle modest beginnings.

When you are focused on a vision and eager to fulfill your deepest objectives, you get impatient to arrive at your destination. That intensifies when combined with anger at your present situation. The risk of hating modest beginnings is that you can lose sight of the importance of the trip. Because you are continually thinking about where you should be, you risk missing lessons that are meant to be learned in your present setting because you aren't giving your current work, business concept, or lack thereof, you're all.

Every stage of your life has importance, and this is the only opportunity you will ever have to learn. Make the most of every chance you are given and utilize it as practice towards your desired outcome.

3. Use your capacity for planning.

If you're ambitious, you should utilize your unease about your present situation as fire for your ambitions. Spend that energy preparing for your next step. Without a strategy for how to enter your next season, it doesn't help to hate your present situation. In other words, while you are where you are, you intend to seek what comes next. The planning for the next stage is currently in progress. Planning is essential because it enables you to create a strategy for the next phase, work actively toward it, and provide you the authority and capacity to alter your situation.

Always in charge, you have the freedom to take advantage of your situation. You need to avoid harboring animosity within you if you want the weight of ambition to work in your favor.

Instead of wishing things were different, use your energy to do something constructive.

You should assess your surroundings to make sure it is supportive in a world that is awash with information and continually makes us feel inadequate. By envying the lives of others and wishing your own were different, you don't gain anything. Focusing on your own life, honing in on your goals, and making an effort to achieve them can provide far greater rewards. While seeing the lives of others might inspire you, the work still has to be done by you.

Ambition only burns when it is improperly controlled.

CONCLUSION

Even though it sounds like an emotion, ambition is an act of faith. Ambition is the choice to see beyond your current situation and choose for a better future. The very reason why desire has such a strong life force is because of this trust. It inspires individuals to think broadly and apply such ideas to surpass their constraints.

Living your greatest life requires an understanding of what ambition is, why you stopped being ambitious, and what to do to overcome your lack of desire. Make sure to keep your attention on the bright side and avoid dreading failure. Just those two simple actions might be the difference between realizing your aspirations and sitting on the sofa and watching them pass you by.

It may take some time to overcome your lack of ambition, especially if you're doing it without the boost of inspiration that comes from being enthusiastic about a new project or idea, but the effort will be worthwhile. You can advance professionally, feel content and prosperous, make more friends, and forge stronger ties with family with the aid of ambition.

In a professional setting, ambition is not necessary. Even at home, you can have high goals. Many individuals discover, for example, that having children causes their desire to resurface or to emerge for the first time. It's all about you, and if you take at least a few of our recommendations into consideration, we are certain that you will be able to achieve your goals.